FREQUENCIES

Other books by Matt Bialer

Radius
Wing of Light
Already Here
Ark
Black Powder
Bridge
Tell Them What I Saw
He Walks On All Fours
Kings of Men
Ascent

FREQUENCIES

Matt Bialer

LEAKY BOOT PRESS

Frequencies
by Matt Bialer

First published in 2015 by
Leaky Boot Press
http://www.leakyboot.com

ISBN: 978-1-909849-16-7

FREQUENCIES

FREQUENCIES

He hears
Scratchings of voice

A voice
A sound
A whisper

Friedrich Jürgenson –

Tall, gaunt man
Silver hair

Born in Odessa
1903

Lives in Sweden now

Painter
Archeologist

Former opera singer

Traces

Scratchings of voice

On his tape recorder

1957
At his summer cottage

MATT BIALER

Always interested
In the human voice

Opera
Bird song

Knows ten languages

Traces

Scratchings of voice

Damages his vocal cords
Gives up singing

Concentrate
Entirely on painting

Moves to Sweden
During the War

Landscapes, still lifes

Portraits of
Wealthy Swedes

City of Stockholm

Visits Pompeii

Wants better access
To buried city

Shows his paintings
To the Vatican

Recognize his talent

Ask him to paint
And catalogue their archeological works

Buried beneath
The holy city

He hears
Scratchings of voice

A voice
A sound
A whisper

Tall, gaunt man
Silver hair

Wanders the ruins
With his easel

Pompeii

The Amphitheatre

Temple of Vespasian

Air scented
With perfume
Of rosemary
Rock roses
Sweet yellow broom

Streaks of
Bright, red poppies

Green and white marble

Ionic columns

Wanders the ruins

Always interested
In the human voice

Pope Pius XII
Sees the results of 4 months' work

Asks Friedrich
To paint a portrait of him

Paints 3 more

Granted full access
To Pompeii

Returns there
Many times to paint

Wanders the ruins
With his easel

The Temple of Apollo
Slight angle
To the axis
Of the Forum

Pedestals of the statues
Still remain

Where originals placed
In the front of the colonnade

But the statues
Long since gone

Gone

He hears
Scratchings of voice

Buys a tape recorder
To record his singing

Starts to notice
Some strange phenomenon

Inexplicable fade-ins
And fade-outs on the tape

Abstract visions
Telepathic messages

Produced by

His highly developed

Aural and visual senses

Sits by dining room table
Clearly awake
And relaxed

Senses that
Something is going to happen

Inner calmness

Long sentences
In English

Appear in his consciousness

Long, phonetic sentences

Words

Not correct English

But in a disfigured
Almost alphabetical way

Completely deformed

He does not hear a voice

A sound
Or a whisper

It is all so soundless

So soundless

Tall, gaunt man
Silver hair
Wanders the ruins
With his easel

It is all so soundless

MATT BIALER

Senses that
Something is going to happen

Spring

His wife and he
Go to the country house

Sunny and warm
Garden blossoms

Fragrant smells

Loves the bird songs

Wants to record them

Secluded location

The big garden
Somewhat going to seed

Closely borders forest
With a lake

An abundance
And variety of birds
Goes to attic

Places tape recorder
And microphone

By open window

Sees a chaffinch
On a branch nearby

Turns on recorder

Checks it
After tape runs five minutes

Senses that
Something is going to happen

What he hears
Is very strange

Roaring or hissing
Static sounds

Like a shower
Hissing

Can hear the bird
But sounds far away

Is the tape defective?

Number of nights later

A new tape
Already dark outside
Half-moon

Shines through window
At an angle

Tape recorder on

Very interested
In this static

This hissing

Observes small
Control lamp on recorder

Flickers orange red

Indicates
Electromagnetic impulses

Being received

Hears nothing though

Dark and quiet
In the room

MATT BIALER

Dark and quiet
Sips of
Soderblandning tea

Starts to become sleepy

Nodding off
Awakens

Something is going to happen

Control lamp

Starts to flash
And twitch

Goes out completely

Starts to flicker again

Something coming on the tape
That one should be able to hear

Flashing stops

Replays the tape

His highly trained ear

Little that he can
Clearly perceive

Hissing

One hour
Of concentrated listening

Getting used
To the disturbing noises

He hears
Scratchings of voice
A voice
A sound

A whisper

Traces

Pleasant male voice

Starts to emerge
From chaos of sound

Emerge

English
With deep conviction

Unusual intonation

Something inaudible

Then a German voice
Without an accent

Sentence comes through

Ungrammatical

Voice says

**TSAR REGION WE MUST
SPRINGTIME SPEAK ABOUT**

Tsar region?

Another voice

**FRIEDRICH
YOU ARE BEING OBSERVED!**

FREIDERICH

The voice calls out

**WHEN YOU TRANSLATE
AND INTERPRET THE GERMAN
DURING THE DAY**

MATT BIALER

TRY TO SOLVE THE TRUTH

EVERY EVENING

WITH THE SHIPS

Hissing sounds

In audible

THE SHIPS IN THE DARK

Hissings

Scratchings of voice

A voice
A sound
A whisper

**FRIEDRICH
YOU ARE BEING OBSERVED**

THE SHIPS IN THE DARK

****

She doesn't want me
To reveal her name

My friend
Who came to me

Grieving

I am Tonya

RPA MS Holistic Women's Health Specialist

By profession

Western medicine
Herbalism
Nutrition
Flower essence therapy

To help women
Heal naturally

I also tutor
Parents of deaf children

In ASL
American Sign Language

She doesn't want me
To reveal her name

Lost her son
22 years old
Boating accident
Long Island Sound

42 foot Catalina Sailboat

4 people abroad

Too close to a channel marker

Snagged its rigging and sail

Causing mast to snap

Killed instantly

Sunglasses cover
Her swollen eyes

Her son
Sandy blond hair

Athletic

Always bear hugged me

Teased that I was his real aunt

Aunt Tonnie

Who loves ya Aunt Tonnie?

MATT BIALER

Who loves ya?

She doesn't want me
To reveal her name

Came to my high rise
Manhattan
Upper west side

Dressed in white
Pace face

Sunglasses cover
Her swollen eyes

Walks slowly

Slowly

To help women
Heal naturally

That's when it all began

I started my research

Attempted to comfort
My close friend

Reassure her

Any little sound

That has not been produced
Or heard by us

ITC

Instrumental Transcommunication

Two radios
Tuned to the static

Between stations

18

So-called white noise

A SW radio
And an AM radio

Tuned to what is called
By ITC experimenters

The Jürgenson Wave
1500 KHz

The frequency
Mostly used

I started my research

Transform small portable radio

Into broadband receiver

Added to the equipment

Sit on the floor

3 radios

The static between stations

Produce the acoustic carrier

Static

White noise

Background sound

For our recording

Same hour of day

Write down our questions beforehand

Date
Hour
Phases of the moon

MATT BIALER

Weather conditions
Our psychological moods

Carefully listen
To the tape

Write down in our log

The static between stations

Any little sound

That has not been produced
Or heard by us

During the recording

Carefully listen
To the tape

Any little sound

One day we hear an odd noise

Little sighs
Muffled breath

Near the microphone

That was when it began

When it began

My cellphone beeps

My older sister

Partner
Prestigious Manhattan law firm

Married
3 kids
Large house in Greenwich

Husband

Partner
Private equities investment firm

Shops at Bergdoff

Latest designs
From Gucci, Lanvin
Dolci and Gabbana

      − How's Henry doing?

That's my 7 year old son

He's good

Should be home
From school any minute now

Born deaf

My sister
Learned to sign

So she can
Communicate with him

My ex-husband refuses to

Says it's too hard
Doesn't want him signing

There is nothing wrong
With being deaf

Should never be made to feel
That something is wrong

      − So, have you found them?

Who?

      − You know who

Our deceased father

MATT BIALER

Brother
Grandparents
The static between stations

I don't want to answer that

Any little sound

      – Why not?

If I ever said yes
Would you believe me?

        – I most definitely would not

Any little sound

That has not been produced
Or heard by us

Henry comes home

I tap him

There is nothing wrong
With being deaf

Deaf children born deaf
Will always be deaf

Sign to him

3 fingers

UP?

American Sign Language
Verbs may agree
With both subject and object

Open 8 handshape

Fingers and thumb
Are spread

With the middle finger
Bent at base joint

All other fingers extended

Pulls out of X –men backpack

Boy doll with malleable hands
And fingers

So that it can sign

I CAN SIGN DOLL

Signs

CHARLIE HIS NAME

I sign

HOW COOL HENRY

CAN I HOLD HIM?

Touch chin
Wave my hand downward

THANK YOU

HELLO CHARLIE

She doesn't want me
To reveal her name

Any little sound

That had not been produced
Or heard by us

Carefully listen to the tape

Any little sound

The static between stations

An odd noise

MATT BIALER

A sigh
Muffled breath

That was when it began

When it began

One day I ask

Is the reason
We have no positive results so far

To protect us
From negative influences?

We rewound the tape

Any little sound

White noise

The static between stations

Sighs

Spanish of some sort

 Faint female voices

In audible

Then a completely different voice

Male

Clear

In English

YOU ARE CORRECT

****

He hears
Scratchings of voice

A voice
A sound
A whisper

Friedrich Jürgenson

Tall, gaunt man
Silver hair

Wanders the ruins
With his easel

Up the Via Consolare

To the Villa of Mysteries

Stunning frescoes
Of the Bacchanalian rites

Road paved with polygonal
Basalt rocks

From the Forum
To the Herculaneum Gate

Air scented
With perfume

Of rosemary
Rock roses
Sweet yellow broom

It is all so soundless

Soundless

One evening

Friedrich again
Sits in front of the tape recorder

Turned on to record

Control lamp lights up

MATT BIALER

Flickers

Stops recording

Listens

Just static
And the hiss

Hiss

Wishes his unknown friends
Would make their voices audible

Instead of the hissing

Traces

Records

Waits

Always interested
In the human voice

Control lamp lights up

Flickers

A voice
A sound
A whisper

Starts to emerge
From the chaos of sound

HOER OUR VOICE

HEAR OUR VOICE

Next night
A new tape

Lets equipment
Record family conversation

Listens later on

Sips of
Soderblandning tea

Whispers

Tracings

Scratchings of voice

German and Swedish simultaneously

One female voice
Stands out clearly

Swedish
With decidedly French accent

But too tired
To listen more

Next day
Plays back whole recording

At a slower speed

A whisper

Clearly audible

Within my recorded voice

A whisper

Tireless woman's voice

Hears word

HELP

Recognize the voice

Childhood

MATT BIALER

He knows her

Knows her

German
Swedish
English
And Italian

Other voices

**Address him as
FABROR PELLE**

Uncle Pelle

Children of his wife
Call him that

That can't be them though

Can hear

**FRIEDRICH
FRIEDEL
FEDERICK
FEDRICO**

What are they?

How do they know my name?

How do they know my name?

Am I going mad?

Are they voices from outer space?

Friedrich Jürgenson

Tall, gaunt man
Silver hair

He hears
Scratchings of voice

28

Wanders the ruins
With his easel

One spring morning

Scratchings of voice

Bird song

La Campania
Is already beginning to warm

Blue sky
Hazy sun

Vesuvius
Innocuous looking mound
To the north

A breeze tousles the greenery

Scent of rosemary

It is all so soundless

So soundless

Ancient roads
Paved with large roughly flat stone

Broken, irregular stone walls
Open to cell-like enclosures

Their homes
And shops

Some tin roofs

Vesuvius
Innocuous looking mound
To the north

He hears
Scractchings of voice

29

During the night

The eruption had
Changed its form

Gas rich magma
From the upper chambers

Became exhausted

Heavy magma
From deeper down

Begins to reach the surface

Violent tremors

Discharge of magma

Shocks ripple
Across the bay

The sea sucked
And hurled back at the beaches

Seismic tidal wave

The Pelean phase
Of the eruption begins

He hears
Scratchings of voice

A voice
A sound
A whisper

His equipment
Runs for awhile

Record mode

Late afternoon
Alone in the studio

Are they from outer space?

Getting ready
To place headphones on

Intense puffing sound

Simultaneously
Through headphones

And in the room

Senses that
Something is going to happen

Feeling of happy certainty

Puffing sound

No doubt be picked up
By the microphone

Sounds unmistakably

Breaths of a person

Unmistakably

Forcefully exhaling

Repeated

Like someone demonstrating
Breathing techniques

Lungs emptied so much

Whistling sound

Bronchial membranes

A German male voice

SO COLD!

MATT BIALER

First sound he hears
In real time

In the room

And on the headphones
Recorded

Breathing

Breaths

And then that female voice
Again

In Swedish

**HELP RADIO FRIEDRICH
HELP RADIO**

Receives a letter
From German publishing company

His childhood friend
Boris Sacharow

Died in a car accident
Wife still in critical condition

A coma in Bayreuth Hospital

Been out of touch with him

For years

Years

Poor Boris

And a copy of published book
By him

The Big Secret

Renowned yoga teacher

In Germany

Countless photos
Of Boris

Shaved head

Different yoga positions

Brings back memories

Shared childhood

Teenage years
Odessa

Fathers both doctors
Worked together

HELP RADIO

Last page of book

Boris practices
Deep breaths

Empties his lungs

Standing there
Pulled in diaphragm

Smiling

Blowing

Piercing blue eyes

Odessa

Jewel of the Black Sea

Lanzheron Beach

So long ago

MATT BIALER

Water fights

So long ago

Blowing

Breathing

Immediately listens
To tapes again

Right at the beginning

Scratchings of voice

Strained
But in audible German

AT EQUIPMENT, YOUR BORIS

Names pronounced painfully

Boeerrissss

HELP US THE RADIO FRIEDRICH

Tall, gaunt man
Silver hair

Wanders the ruins
With his easel

Triangular colonnade

Housing the oldest temple
In the city

The Amphitheatre
And the Great Palestra

Athletic games and sports
130 by 140 meters

A pool surrounded
By two rows of trees

34

Relief from the sun

Traces of the roots can be seen

Forum Baths
Macellum

3 restored marble columns
From the particle

With Corinthian capitals

Remain standing
In front of the façade

The Temple of Isis

It is all so soundless

So soundless

He hears
The scracthings of voice

A voice
A sound
A whisper

One day
While recording

Friedrich has
A major breakthrough

Fundamentally alters
His view on the voices

When he plays
Back the recording

FRIEDEL, CAN YOU HEAR ME?

FRIEDEL?

MATT BIALER

Her pet nickname for him

It is Mammy

He hears the voice
Of his dead mother

Speaking directly to him

Directly to him

YOU LOVE, YOU LIVE IN LOVE
IN ME LIVES ELLY, FRIEDEL LIVES
YOU LIVE...WE LIVE

ELLY, FRIEDEL PAPA LIVES
MANY LIVE...ALAS, ALAS
YOU LOVE HELEN

Plays the recording
To his wife and sister Elly

They recognize the voice

Recognize the voice

And agree that content
On the magnetic tape

Must be message
From beyond the grave

****

My friend

Who doesn't want me
To reveal her name

Stops attending the experiments

No sign of her son

No sign

36

Any little sound

That has not been produced
Or heard by me

Radios
Tuned to the static

Between stations

The Jürgenson Frequency

So-called white noise

Provides
An acoustic carrier

From which our communicators

Supposedly modulate
Or construct their own voices

Procedure involved in
EVP

Electronic Voice Phenomenon

Is simple

Construct their own voices

Offers no mystery

Experimenter turns on recorder
And the radio

Addresses a question

Such as

Can anyone hear me?

To the communicator

Hopes may be present

Experimenter then remains silent
For a minute or two

While tape or digital recorder

Continues to record
The white noise

Another question is then asked

Procedure then repeated
For ten minutes

Same time of day

If I travel to a conference
I take the equipment with me

Same time of day

Any little sound

That has not been produced
Or hear by me

Radios
Tuned to the static

Between stations

Construct their own voices

Play back the recording
On my laptop

Wear headphones

Electro-acoustic process software

Sound Forge

Hope to hear
Faint anomalous voice

Muffled breath

Whispers

Frequently nothing is heard

May take a week

Months

Patient and regular
Recording sessions

If and when voices do occur
Usually give 2 or 3 word replies

Another extraordinary ITC phenomenon
Made its appearance

Another channel of communication

Allows for lengthier dialogue

DRV

Direct Radio Voices

Allows apparent communicator
To interact with the experimenter

By speaking through the loudspeaker
Of a radio

In real time

Anyone present in the room
During the session

Can listen to
And even put questions

To the communicator

Construct their own voices

The static between stations

MATT BIALER

Any little sound

That has not been produced
Or heard by me

There is nothing so stunning
And moving

Nothing

For the experimenter

As these incredible voices

That can sound loud and clear
In his/her own house

And answer the questions

Nothing so stunning
And moving

**THERE IS AN ABYSS
IN THE OTHER WORLD**

"Another world" frequently repeated

When I ask who is speaking

ANOTHER WORLD

**THE DEAD SPEAK
WE CREATE THE CONTACT**

**DIFFICULT
IT IS DIFFICULT**

MAKE VOICE

Spoken by several
Masculine and feminine voices

I ask them
If they can hear me

**WE ARE LISTENING
TO EVERYTHING**

WE ARE HERE WITH YOU

EXTREMELY DIFFICULT

TIME STREAM

LIKE A RADIO

What is Time Stream?

No sign of her son

No sign

Ask to speak
To a member of my family

Especially my father

Complain to the voices
That I thought

My father would
Speak to me sooner

He would try

THAT IS WHAT YOU ASSUME

One day
I hear my brother's voice

Anomalous voice

Died of cancer at 37

And at last my father

Pronounces his name loudly
And clearly

A number of times

MATT BIALER

TONYA IT IS DAD

CAN YOU HEAR ME

TONYA

THE RUINS RISE
TONYA

THE RUINS RISE

Was a Roman history professor

Did not believe in the paranormal

Though had premonition
Of own sudden death

Construct their own voices

I realize that he tried
To speak to me

From the first months
Of my experiments

THE RUINS RISE

Strange shouts

Unpleasant guttural noises

A machine

After my thousands of hours
Of listening to anomalous voices

I can hear his voice
In the harsh noise

The static between stations

IT IS YOUR FATHER SPEAKING

Another landmark

42

The day I hear a voice

Says it is my grandmother

Identifies itself
As my beloved grandmother

**THE HOUSE IS SO NICE
TONYA**

SMELLS OF ROSEMARY

So beautiful
This house in next world

IT IS TOO MUCH FOR ME

TOO MUCH

I remember her cottage
Abutting Cape Cod National Seashore

Woodlands

Entered from a small farmer's porch
Into the living room

Gas stove/fireplace

Smell of rosemary

HOW IS LULU?

Who is Lulu?

HOW IS DEAR LULU?

**DON'T KNOW HOW
TO SPEAK WITH ME
ANY LONGER**

Smell of rosemary

I pick up Henry
From school

MATT BIALER

Sign

WHAT'S UP?

ME TEACHER ORANGE GIVE

Finger in palm
For SHOW

ASL

Verbal agreement
Aspectual marking

Productive system
Of forming agglutinative classifiers

Subject-verb-object

ME ANOTHER DOLL WANT

Another

I CAN SIGN DOLL

WHY?

A FRIEND

A FRIEND

My ex-husband
Refuses to learn ASL

Cannot communicate
With him

Doesn't want him to
Sign either

Not useful
In the real world

Too difficult

Just deaf friends

Doesn't feel natural

Wants him to get surgery

CI
Cochlear Implant

So he can experience
Sound world

Learn to speak

Construct their own voices

Deafness is not a disability
It is a different way of being

You listen to your dead people

Why can't he have a chance like that?

It doesn't often work

They're not really hearing

Sensory confusion

There is nothing wrong
With being deaf

Deaf children born deaf
Will always be deaf

It's in his best interests

He'll be able to speak

Construct their own voices

It's just impressions

You cannot make a
Born deaf child

45

MATT BIALER

Comprehend sounds

Any more than
A born blind child
Appreciate color

No real concept of sound
Let alone speech

The implants often fail

It's alien

When he is old enough
He can make his own decision

I don't want him signing

No real concept of sound

The CI isn't going to unscramble that

You listen to your dead people

Far better to give
A child immediate access

To sign language

Use that as foundation
To proceed

Construct their own voices

You listen to your dead people

We can argue forever

Listen to my dead people

I speak to my sister
On the phone

Unload my frustrations

— Don't let him stop
— Henry from signing

— He'll never have a grasp of language

— If you let him stop it

Do you know what Lulu means?

— What did you say?

Lulu
What does it mean?

— Lulu? Grandma

What?

— That was her pet nickname for me
— It was our little secret
— I was her Lulu

— Our little secret

I remember her
Chasing me through Grandma's cottage

Glow of sunburn
At the end of the day

Lobster dinners

Dragged every summer morning
To Red Cross swimming lessons

Frigid Nantucket Sound

The house's big trestle dining table

Fishing off the beach
With Grandpa

For striped bass

We hated taking the fish off the hooks

MATT BIALER

And the worms

   – Why did you ask about Lulu?

Listen to my dead people

Any little sound

That has not been produced
Or heard by me

The static between stations

So-called white noise

Wear headphones
Electro-acoustic processing software

Sound Forge

A new voice
Pablo

Becomes my new friend
My guide

SPEAKING FROM TIME STREAM STATION

**ZEISTRM IN GERMAN
RIO DE TEMPO IN PORTUGUESE**

THE BRIDGE BETWEEN WORLDS

A TOWER

What are you?

Where are you?

A RADIO TOWER

THE BRIDGE BETWEEN WORLDS

IN THE UNIVERSE NOTHING PERISHES

IT SIMPLY CHANGES SHAPE

**I AM PABLO
FROM TIME STREAM STATION**

**TOWER TOWER
IT IS TIME STREAM**

**THE UNIVERSE
IS DREAMT BY THE VOID**

****

He hears
Scratchings of voice

A voice
A sound
A whisper

Friedrich Jürgenson

Tall, gaunt man
Silver hair

Wanders the ruins
With his easel

A fearful black cloud

Forked and quivering
Bursts of flame

Great tongue of fire

Soon afterward
The cloud sank to earth

Five to six minutes
To reach Pompeii

From the top of the crater

A dense rolling
Ground-hugging mass
Of gas, ash and rock

MATT BIALER

The pyroclastic flow

Preceded a few second later
By a scorching blast

Like that of a flame thrower

Walls thrown down
Columns toppled

Tiles shot like cannon balls
Down the streets

He enters
The Garden of the Fugitives

Air scented
With perfume

Of rosemary
Rock roses
Sweet yellow broom

It is all so soundless

So soundless

He hears
Scratchings of voice

A voice
A sound
A whisper

He finally understands
What the voice called Lena

Has been telling him to do

MAKE CONTACT WITH THE RADIO

Hook up the tape recorder
With the radio receiver

MAKE CONTACT WITH THE RADIO

Notice right away
With use of headphones

Can hear broadcasts

Overwhelmed
By the chaos of sounds and noises

Within the music, theater,
Performances, singing, lectures
And droning

Can hear Lena's whispering

Cannot understand
How her voice

Could be among
The radio broadcasts

But it is

Her disembodied voice

Hard to make out the words
From her hurried whispering

Turns the tape recorder
On record

For a test

Let the tape run
A few minutes

Hook up to the radio

Lena's voices
Suddenly comes through clearly

In the noise

MATT BIALER

51

Turn the radio knob

Back and forth
Different frequencies

Broadcasts
The Symphony

Bits and pieces
Of words and sentences

FRIEDEL FRIEDEL

Sings a voice

Clear emphasis
On the last syllable

The strange mix
Of German and Swedish

Follows Lena's voice

Simultaneously
In two languages

**SPEAK LATELY SWEDISH
OFTEN DISTURBS**

Turns the knob
To another frequency

Same woman's voice

Audible

And drowning out
All other voices

**PLEASE DON'T INTERUPT
FEDERICO**

Sentences in German

Can still recognize
Slavic accent

His way of turning knob
His way of recording

Is disturbing

Next time
He turns the radio on

Set to frequency

1445-1500 KHz

Again the voice
Several languages

German, Italian Swedish

BAMBINA ARRIVA

ARRIVA!

In Italian
Great emotion

**THROUGH THE RADIO
YOU HAVE GUESSED IT**

MUCH MORE WILL COME THROUGH

THROUGH THE RADIO

MUCH MORE

Friedrich realizes
That he has discovered a bridge

A bridge

Unimaginable possibilities

Now after much trial and error

MATT BIALER

A new border

A bridge connected
To an unknown world

A tower

A plane of existence
That until now

Had been closed
For the rest of us

Closed for the rest of us

He wanders the ruins
With his easel

Tall, gaunt man
Silver hair

Volcanic ash
And pumice

Rained down
For 18 hours

Depths of
8 to 10 feet

Explosive superheated
Pyroclastic clouds

Of toxic gas and debris
In six surges

City buried
For 1600 years

When rediscovered
They found holes in the ash

Revealing the forms

Of many of the deceased

Suffocated by volcanic gases
Covered in ash and debris

Their bodies eventually decayed
Inside the hardening matter

Just their shapes left

Scientists blew plaster
Into the holes

Let dry overnight

Remove the ash
Around the hole

Discover human statue

Sarcophagus of ash
Imprints of each body

Crouching
Writhing
Huddled

Horror and agony
In the death throes

It is all so soundless

So soundless

He wander the ruins
With his easel

Stands at the entrance
Of the Garden of the Fugitives

Just their shapes left

He hears
Scratchings of voice

A voice
A sound
A whisper

Now he has a collaborator
Claude Thorlis

Records hundreds of tapes

Refers to the voices
As his invisible friends

Recording of over 140 deceased relatives
Close friends and others

Summer of 1963
Decides to make his research public

Invites press
To first of many international press conferences
In Molnbo

Always interested in the human voice

Prior to conference

Chief engineer
Of Swedish National Public Broadcasting

Inspects recording equipment

Assures audience

It has not been manipulated,
Tampered with,
Modified

In any way

Friedrich insists

Judge the phenomenon
With an open

Yet critical mind

To avoid possible deception
Including self-deception

Urges people to form
Small research groups

Make recordings jointly

With the cooperation
And presence

Of acoustic experts
Radio engineers
Experts in electronics
Parapsychologists

During the conference
Journalist from newspaper **Aftonbladet**

Confronts Friedrich

To acknowledge
That these are voices
Of unknown origin on tape

Is one thing

But to insist
That the voices

Are from beyond the grave
Is something quite different

It is preposterous

Maybe not until
You yourself hear a voice

That is clearly
Identifiable as a friend
Or close relative

MATT BIALER

Maybe then

Judge the phenomenon
With an open

Yet critical mind

It is preposterous

He hears
Scratchings of voice

A voice
A sound
A whisper

Pled for journalists
Acoustic experts
Other researchers

But fails
To be a catalyst

For systematic
And thorough scientific research
On Electronic Voice Phenomenon

Despite publicity
Positive testimony
From widely known experts

No one from
Scientific community

Steps forward

No one

To keep costs low

My wife and I
Will put our cottage
In the forest

Four rooms
Kitchen
And bath

At disposal of researchers
As an experimental
Residential community

That is all I can do

All I can offer

But the offer
Is not accepted

Turned off
By his absolute conviction

That the voices
Were undisputable, objective proof

Of life after death

And the language
Spoken on the tapes

Makes it hard
For scientists to
Take phenomenon seriously

The mix of German, English,
Russian, Swedish, Italian

Often combining
Several languages

A striking coincidence
That Friedrich knows

All of these languages

A striking coincidence

MATT BIALER

Judge the phenomenon
With an open

Yet critical mind

It is preposterous

It is a projection
Of his own mind

Some form
Of telekinesis

How could I project
Voices onto tape?

Tell me how?

That would be fascinating
In itself

Friedrich's own writings

The voices
Trying to establish contact

With his poodle

Come through stronger
During a full moon

These presences can make
An appearance on our own televisions screens

Seems odd and humorous
To empirically oriented scientists

It is preposterous

Judge the phenomenon
With an open

Yet critical mind

He hears
Scratchings of voice

A voice
A sound
A whisper

Discovers the simple truth

Biggest difficulties
And obstacles

Are to be found
Within ourselves

And without their removal

Attempted approach
By the invisible dimension of life

Will not be realized

Will inevitably lead
To new misunderstanding

Will not be realized

We don't need
Just a radio

These presences

Can make an appearance

On our television screens

Our television screens

We don't need
Just a radio

WE LIVE! WE!
AYE FRIEDEL!

MATT BIALER

**THE DEAD LIVE
SINCE THEY ARE NOT DEAD**

WE ARE HUMANS

THE DEAD ARE HUMANS

****

Any little sound

That has not been produced
Or heard by me

Radios
Tuned to the static

Between stations

The Jürgenson Frequency

So-called white noise

Provides
An acoustic carrier

From which our communicators

Supposedly modulate
Or construct their own voices

Construct their own voices

Play back the recording
On my laptop

Wear headphones

Electro-acoustic process software

Sound Forge

Hope to hear
Faint anomalous voices

Muffled breath

Whispers

Construct their own voices

My friend Pablo

From Time Stream

ANOTHER WORLD

THE DEAD SPEAK
WE CREATE THE CONTACT

DIFFICULT
IT IS DIFFICULT

MAKE VOICE

TIME STREAM

IT IS A STATION

I ask a lot of questions

DEATH IS SO BEAUTIFUL

IT IS ONLY UGLY
IN SPACE

Space time

Time Stream

Where is your world?

Ask question repeatedly

Without getting a response

One evening
When I ask the same question

A loud, authoritative voice
Suddenly interrupts

MATT BIALER

**NOT TO THAT
NOT TO THAT QUESTION**

Descriptions of their world
Not easily obtained

**A WORLD VERY SIMILAR
TO YOURS**

IT IS GOOD

**IT IS THE GATE
TO THE LIGHT**

IT IS BEAUTIFUL HERE

Pablo

Very powerful, masculine voice

Speaks with me everyday

Won't answer

Who he is

Or was

Distinctive timbre expressions

Jokes with me

Playfully invites me

DANCE THE TANGO

Patient with my questions

Everyday

Same time of day

Taping sessions
Not too long

Not more than 10 or 15 minutes

For the recording

4 to 5 questions

Usually replies
With yes or no

Everyday

DO NOT LOSE OUR CONTACTS

Time Stream

A radio station

Grammar oddities

The language of the dead

Pictorial language
Of the subconscious

Difficulties in
Constructing their own voices

Difficulties

Many of the words
Cannot be understood

Unintelligible

Anomalous voices

Interspersed with long silences

Sometimes clear
Other times distorted

Tremulous echoes

Tracings

Any little sound

MATT BIALER

That has not been produced
Or heard by us

The static between stations

So-called white noise

Construct their own voices

The son of my friend

Who doesn't want me
To reveal her name

No sign of him

No sign

I ask but
Do not receive a reply

I ask if they
Can see our world

ONLY SOME CAN

A LOT OF WORK

TO SPEAK

TO SEE

Time Stream

A station in the next world

**CAN SEND CONTACTS
FROM OUR STATION**

EXTREMELY DIFFICULT PROCESS

WE HAVE A BODY

A MUCH MORE BEAUTIFUL BODY

MUCH MORE FLEXIBLE

MADE OF KIND OF ELECTRICTY

WE ARE DEAD

THE EARTH IS A SMUDGED COPY

**OF THE WORLD
IN WHICH WE DWELL**

THE EARTH IS A SMUDGED COPY

One day
When I ask Pablo how he is

BE LEAVING SOON

Where are you leaving to?

LEAVING SOON

But where Pablo?

Where?

**TONYA IT IS DAD
CAN YOU HEAR ME?**

TONYA

**THE RUINS RISE
TONYA**

THE RUINS RISE

Construct their own voices

Strange shouts

Unpleasant guttural noises

I can hear his voice
In the harsh noise

THE RUINS RISE

The static between stations

MATT BIALER

IT IS YOUR FATHER SPEAKING

I hear grandmother again

**THE HOUSE IS SO BEAUTIFUL
TONYA**

**SMELL THE ROSEMARY
THE ROSEMARY**

IT IS ALMOST TOO MUCH

HOW IS DEAR LULU?

OH LULU

WILL YOU TELL HER?

I burn a cd
Of this recording

And others of my father, brother
Grandparents

Next time
I talk to my sister

      − How is Henry?

I don't know

*He's with his father
This weekend*

*And that always
Makes me nervous*

*Still going on
About the implant*

      − Does he tell Henry that?

No

He would if he could sign

68

I don't know why
He doesn't want to converse with him

He wants to converse
But on his terms

> – Tonya
> – Why did you ask me about Lulu?

> – Did you know that nickname?

No, I never did

Look for a package I sent you

It contains a cd

Listen to it
Then we'll talk

Please listen to it

Henry comes home
From weekend with my Ex

Dark, wavy hair
X-Men backpack

He looks sad

Sign to him

3 fingers

WHAT'S UP?

He doesn't answer

Sign again

WHAT'S UP?

Nods his head

Signs

69

Closed fist
With index finger extended

DISAPPOINTED

Won't tell me more

Leave him alone

Later in his room
I find his two I CAN SIGN dolls

Nick and Preston

Blue shirts
Brown and blue eyes

Crouched together

Holding each other

DISAPPOINTED

Any little sound

That has not been produced
Or heard by me

The static between stations

So-called white noise

Provides
An acoustic carrier

From which our communicators

Supposedly modulate
Or construct their own voices

Construct their own voices

Time Stream

One of the voices

70

SO WE HAVE NEW EQUIPMENT HERE

I bought a new mixing table

Construct their own voices

TO MODULATE THE WAVES

WE ONLY NEED SHORT WAVES

More than one radio

Rich mixture of frequencies
To choose from

Common aspect of
Many anomalous voices

An increase in speed
In comparison to normal
Human voices

THIS IS TIME STREAM

THIS IS THE RIVER OF THE WHOLE
THIS IS THE RIVER OF THE ALL

THIS IS TIME STREAM

Ask me to leave
All of my machines on

Even if I am not there

Sometimes ask me to turn off
My cell phone

Interferes

Practicing voices

WE ARE WORKING

WE CANNOT SPEAK TO YOU
TODAY

MATT BIALER

71

I hear them repeat
For hours

WE ARE ALL DEAD

TIME STREAM

WE ARE ALL DEAD

**FROM TEMPO, AUNT,
FATHER, NOVEMBER**

Also repeat

**ALPHA BETA
ALPHA BETA
ALPHA BETA**

Repetitions heard
All night

All day

Interspersed with
Clear, strong voices

Or blurred
And distorted

WE ARE THE DEAD

WE ARE THE DEAD

I ask them about Pablo

I have not heard his voice
In some time

NO LONGER IN TIME STREAM'S WORLD

**MOVED INTO A WORLD
THAT IS LIKE THE SUN**

**A WORLD FROM WHICH
HE CANNOT SPEAK**

PABLO IS IN THE SUN

He is in the sun?
What do you mean?

**IT IS NOT YOUR SUN
BUT IT IS A SUN**

HE IS IN THE SUN

THE EARTH IS A SMUDGED COPY

****

He hears
Scratchings of voice

A voice
A sound
A whisper

Friedrich Jürgenson

Tall. Gaunt man
Silver hair

Oct. 15, 1987
Dies at age 84

While the funeral
Is taking places

Village church
In Hoor six days later

Friedrich's dear friend
And collaborator Claude Thorlis

Sits in his home
In Eskilstuna 500 kilometers away

As he was instructed to
By Friedrich

MATT BIALER

During breakfast
That same morning

Claude's wife Ellen

Thinks she hears

A loud and clear inner voice

Repeats

CHANNEL 4

CHANNEL 4

CHANNEL 4

Distinct feeling
That it may

Have something to do
With funeral

Claude immediately
Starts thinking

Of radio and television

But only 3 channels
Broadcasting on the radio

And 2 on television

CHANNEL 4

When the funeral
Starts at 1 pm

Turns on the television

Put on Channel 4

Screen snowy
Electrical noise

74

22 minutes
Into the ceremony

Small glimmer of light

Flickers on the buzzing dark screen

Claude takes out
His Polaroid camera

Snaps photograph
Of the screen

As the picture
Develops before their eyes

A white figure
Floats up

Against black monitor

Swims

Before their eyes

Contours
Of ghostly white figure

Swims

Starts to emerge

Become clear

Ellen gasps

Herregud!

Oh my God!

Herregud!

Det ar Friedel!

It is Friedel!

Friedel

****

Radio
Tuned to the static

Between stations

The Jürgenson Frequency

So-called white noise

Provides
An acoustic carrier

From which our communicators

Supposedly modulate
Or construct their own voices

Construct their own voices

WE ARE WORKING

WE CANNOT SPEAK TO YOU TODAY

WE ARE THE DEAD

ALL DEAD HERE

TIME STREAM

WE ARE THE DEAD

TIME STREAM

**AUNTIE, UNCLE
THANK YOU**

THIS IS THE RIVER OF THE WHOLE

THIS IS THE RIVER OF THE ALL

THIS IS TIME STREAM

ALPHA BETA

Repetitions heard
All day and night

THE EARTH IS A SMUDGED COPY

TIME STREAM A BRIDGE

A BRIDGE

Any little sound

That has not been produced
Or heard by me

I have recorded anomalous voices

Using other sources of noise

Radio emissions in foreign languages

Running water

Soft wind
In the trees

Chants

Traffic noise

Birds singing
In the open air

I hear the guttural noise

Hurried whispering

Scratches of voice

Tracings

But in my experience

It is the white noise

MATT BIALER

Originating directly from the radios

That provides
Best conditions for contact

Best conditions

The Jürgenson Frequency

Static between stations

One day
I hear noise

Hurried whispers

High pitched squeaks
Almost human

WHO LOVES YA AUNT TONNIE?

AUNT TONNIE?

WHO LOVES YA?

****

Friedrich Jürgenson

Tall, gaunt man
Silver hair

Wanders the ruins
With his easel

Enters
The Garden of the Fugitives

Air scented
With perfume

Of rosemary
Rock roses
Sweet yellow broom

It is all so soundless

So soundless

This was an area of vineyards
With outdoor triclinium for summer eating

Stone walls

Thirteen hollow spaces

Found in the hardened layers
Of ash and volcanic debris

Spaces filled with plaster
Became the statues of thirteen people

Largest number of victims
Found in one site

From position in the ash

Determined that they had died
Early in the morning

Of the second day of the eruption

As they attempted to flee the city

The Garden of the Fugitives

Examines the plaster mummies

Of two farm families

And a merchant's family

When they started to flee

First came a servant
Carrying on his shoulder

A bag
Hastily filled with provisions

MATT BIALER

Find him where he fell

Near wall
Of the vegetable garden

Next hand in hand
Farmer's two little boys

4 and 5 years old

Farmer supporting
His trembling wife

Crouching

Lying down

Huddled

Behind farmer's family

A young farm couple
And their daughter

Vague outline

Slender, undernourished child

The Merchant's family

Two young boys
In their teens

Followed by mother
And younger sister

The final figure
In the pageant of death

Is the merchant himself

Friedrich smiles
As he looks at him

Smiles

Not lying down
Like the others

Not lying down

But sitting upright

Arm pressed
Against a mound of earth

And his back bent

In a supreme effort
To get back up

Get back up